MW00632879

ACKNOWLEDGMENTS

I am in awe of the families of individuals with autism. They are tireless in their advocacy and courageous in their efforts not only to help their own children but to support and encourage others. To them I owe a special thanks, especially the Gonyea Family, one and all. My first two students with autism, Jenny and Michael, were my best teachers and will always hold a special place in my heart.

I have been fortunate over the years to have worked with wonderful special educators who inspired and encouraged me. Gail Schenkman and Lynn Sarda, the master teachers who started me on this path, were models of compassion and skill. Faye Cartmell and Lynne Sangaline, both extraordinary and creative teachers, shared the challenges and the joy in each step and never faltered in their ability to see the best in every child. I am also grateful to the dedicated staff at The Children's Annex who provided feedback and assisted in the field-testing and refining of these checklists.

Basic Skills Checklists © 2008 Marlene Breitenbach

basic skills CHECKLISTS

Teacher-friendly assessment for students with autism or special needs

Marlene Breitenbach M.S.Ed., BCBA

Basic Skills Checklists

All marketing and publishing rights guaranteed to and reserved by

FUTURE HORIZONS INC.
721 W. Abram Street
Arlington, Texas 76013
800-489-0727
817-277-0727
817-277-2270 (fax)
E-mail: info@FHautism.com
www.FHautism.com

© Copyright 2000 Marlene Breitenbach M.S.Ed., BCBA

All rights reserved.

Printed in the United States of America.

Future Horizons grants the purchaser of this book permission to make copies of this material if and only if ALL of the following conditions apply:

1) Material is intended for educational purposes.
2) Copies do not exceed fifty (50) per page in the period of one year.
3) Material is not intended for publication or sale of any kind.

For all other copyright permission inquiries, please contact the Editor: info@FHautism.com.

ISBN 10: 1-932565-75-2
ISBN 13: 978-1-932565-75-1

CONTENTS

READING AND LANGUAGE ARTS

MATH

FINE MOTOR

INDEPENDENCE

PARENT CHECKLISTS

INTRODUCTION

Educators serving children with autism and other special needs are challenged to provide individualized and effective programs whether in public or private school and more often in the context of full inclusion classrooms. Knowing that good teaching begins with appropriate assessment, teachers need an efficient and effective means of determining current skills and monitoring progress.

The Basic Skills Checklists were created over many years in the classroom and have proven useful in identifying and prioritizing objectives. When used prior to teaching and for regular reviews, the checklists allow us to monitor the effectiveness of our teaching and provide a record of the child's progress.

Since only specific sections relevant for each child are administered, the tool is flexible. Additional checklists can be administered over a period of time as new objectives are targeted. Most checklists are designed to be used for both individual or small group administration.

As children transition from one grade or classroom to another, sharing *Basic Skills Checklists* with the receiving teacher helps ensure continuity in programming.

DESCRIPTION

Basic Skills Checklists is an informal, curriculum-based assessment tool designed for use with preschool and elementary-aged special needs children. Each checklist focuses on separate skill areas in the following domains.

- Basic Concepts
- Reading
- Language Arts
- Math
- Fine Motor
- Writing
- Independence

The skill areas selected are not intended to be all-inclusive, but rather are meant to give an overall view of functioning in the home or school environment and identify possible objectives to be addressed in the curriculum. The checklist can be used as a tool to zero in on a child's current skills, so that instruction can begin at an appropriate level. The manual includes guidelines for administration and task presentation, interpretation of the results, and sample checklists and blank forms.

A Special Educator or classroom teacher may administer the checklist after reviewing the administration guidelines that follow. With the guidance of the teacher, the checklist can also be administered by a paraprofessional who is familiar with the child. Selected sections are intended to be completed by parents.

ADMINISTRATION

INDIVIDUAL AND GROUP ADMINISTRATION

While the majority of the checklists are designed for assessment on an individual basis, some can also be administered to small groups of children. This can be more efficient, as up to nine children can be tracked on a single sheet. The administration options are noted in the upper right-hand corner of each checklist as "I" (Individual Administration) or "I/G" (Individual or Group Administration).

Individual administration is recommended for tasks that involve discrimination learning. Group administration can be more efficient if several children need to be assessed and the target skill is one of "whole task" completion. For example, receptive identification of letters or number sequencing might be better conducted on an individual basis, whereas cutting skills, clothing fasteners, and work skills can be done with a small group.

CHECKLIST SELECTION

Basic Skills Checklists covers a range of skills, from readiness level to age-appropriate skills for young elementary children.

The teacher should first select the relevant checklist to be used for each child. A recent progress note, report card or IEP update can be used as a guide for selecting the domain to be assessed. Keep in mind that the child may have lost or gained skills since the last review. In addition, if the child has recently made a transition from another program or grade, it may be important to check the last-reported mastered skills to ensure that they have generalized to the new setting and materials. If appropriate, base selections on the outcomes targeted in the grade level curriculum.

Basic Skills Checklists can be used with one child to provide an ongoing record. Selected pages may be flagged or highlighted to indicate current assessment areas for that child. If used with a group of children, record responses for all students on a single checklist form, then copy the results to place in each child's portfolio. (See sample group and individual checklists in Appendix.)

Basic Skills Checklists © 2008 Marlene Breitenbach

All items within each checklist should be administered unless there is certainty that the child has mastered all components of that skill area. Sub-sections will include several levels of skills for one concept. For example, in the math area, skills begin with rote counting and include number identification, matching number to quantity, and beginning addition. If the child's IEP documents beginning addition skills, it is not necessary to recheck identification of numbers. If you are unsure about the child's skills in a particular area, start assessment at a level you are sure the child has mastered and continue until you find the level at which the child is unable to demonstrate consistent accuracy.

Note that many skills are assessed both receptively and expressively since these skills may not develop evenly and may need to be specifically taught. Receptive skills target the child's understanding of a concept and are usually demonstrated non-verbally by pointing, showing or giving an item. Expressive skills illustrate the child's ability to label or describe a concept and are demonstrated verbally or using an assistive communication device (e.g., “Point to red” vs. “What color is it?”)

TIMING

The initial administration can occur in the first few weeks of the school year. Periodic rechecks can be done to correspond with school reporting periods or IEP updates. For young children or children who are not yet independent in their personal care, the “Self-Care” checklists (see pp. 41-46) can be sent home to parents to complete and return. The School Skills checklist is also useful to administer at the beginning of the school year and can be used to monitor the child's increasing independence, particularly upon entering Grade 1 or making a transition to a new grade or school.

TASK PRESENTATION

Place the child’s name, the date, and class at the top of each subsection to be administered. Fill in the administrator's name on the appropriate line.

Make sure all necessary materials are easily accessible. On the table, place only the materials that are needed for the specific skill to be checked.

On some checklists, a verbal instruction has been suggested for use with assessment of a specific skill. These are noted in the “comments” section of each form and are examples of clear, simplified directions that may assist the child in understanding what you are asking. In addition, if different staff members administer the checklist over time, consistent instructions will increase the accuracy of the measurement. If no direction is specified, give a short, specific, verbal direction that clearly identifies the task without extraneous language. (For example, “Wash the dishes,” as opposed to “Let's go over to the sink and wash those dirty dishes.”)

After giving the direction, the evaluator should *delay before offering assistance* to make sure the child has the opportunity to initiate task completion on his/her own. After the child's response without assistance has been noted, repeat the direction with help (gestural, physical, or verbal prompt). If the child is successful when the prompt is offered, the skill is an emerging—but not yet mastered—skill.

Some tasks will require several trials or presentations to ensure that there is a clear picture of the child's performance. For example, wiping the table may need to be only observed once; however, color identification may need several repetitions of the task to provide the necessary information.

Observe the child's response and note the score in the appropriate box, using the scoring code. If particular targets are *not* assessed, leave these blank. Only the letter codes designated should be used in scoring. If additional information would be helpful, notes can be added in the "comment" section or logged and dated on the back of the checklist form.

Scoring Code

1.	Correct (C)	=	child gives the correct response with no assistance
2.	Emerging (E)	=	child needs additional cues (physical, gestural, or verbal) to complete the task, but makes attempts
3.	Incorrect (I)	=	child responds incorrectly or makes no attempt, even with prompts

REVIEWING RESULTS

After the selected checklists are completed for each child:

1. Review each checklist to ensure that all relevant sections have been completed. Identify any additional skills that may be appropriate to assess.

2. Identify emerging skills, which will then be addressed as first objectives, making sure the child has the prerequisite skills.

3. Prioritize which objectives will be taught initially. Consider the usefulness of the skill (to the child) and whether enough opportunities for practice can occur. Whenever possible, select skills that are "pivotal," or will lead to the acquisition of other skills, or benefit the child in other ways. For example, learning to ask for help will result in needs being met in several environments. Learning number concepts is a prerequisite for higher-level math

skills. Understanding sequencing is needed for reading comprehension.

4. Compare checklist results to current IEP objectives (if applicable) to check for continuity.

5. Select the program/procedure that will be used to teach each objective, and determine how progress will be monitored or data collected.

6. Select initial target(s) for each objective (e.g., if the objective is receptive color identification, select the first color to teach).

7. Before starting instruction, measure the child's success without assistance with the specific target or set of targets (e.g., identifying the target color).

MATERIALS SELECTION

Since children with special needs, especially children with autism, often have difficulty organizing tasks and understanding verbal directions, it is important to create a structure that will offer them support without compromising the accuracy of the assessment. The following supports are suggested:

- When tasks involve discrimination, make sure the materials differ only in the target variable. (For example, color identification using plastic cups that are identical in every way except color).

- Materials should be familiar to the child, be potentially useful in future environments, and age-appropriate.

- Have the correct number of corresponding parts available for each task, so there is a clear beginning and end (e.g., 5 bottoms, 5 tops).

- Place task components in baskets or bins for easy accessibility.

- Set tasks up clearly so the child can work from left to right to complete the task.

- When discrimination tasks are being assessed, it is important to present at least three choices and several opportunities to demonstrate the skill.

- For receptive tasks, remove all choices between attempts and re-present in random order.

Name: ______________________ Grade: ______________

Date(s) assessed: ______________ School Year: __________

Skill Area: MATCHING Targets:									
IDENTICAL									
Object-to-object									
Picture-to-picture (of object)									
Picture-to-picture (of action)									
Object-to-outline									
Object-to-picture									
Picture-to-object									
Colors (8)									
Shapes (8)									
Uppercase letters									
Lowercase letters									
Numbers									
Words									

Comments:

Code: C = Correct, Independent
E = Emerging or Prompted
I = Incorrect or No Response

Staff Completing Assessment

____

Basic Skills Checklists © 2008 Marlene Breitenbach

Basic Skills Checklist I

Name: ______________________ Grade: ______________

Date(s) assessed: ______________ School Year: ______________

Skill Area: MATCHING Targets:									
NON-IDENTICAL **									
Object-to-object									
Picture-to-picture (of object)									
Picture-to-picture (of action)									
Picture-to-object									
Object-to-picture									
Object-to-picture symbol									
Picture symbol-to-object									

Comments: ** Non-identical items are visually similar but not identical (e.g., different kinds of apples or different types of balls).

Code: C = Correct, Independent
E = Emerging or Prompted
I = Incorrect or No Response

Staff Completing Assessment

____

Name: ______________________________ Grade: ____________________

Date(s) assessed: ____________________ School Year: _______________

Skill Area: SORTING Targets:									
Sorts two sets of objects (Ex: markers, cars)									
Sorts four sets of objects (Ex: markers, cars, blocks, cups)									
Sorts two sets by color (Ex: blue blocks, red blocks)									
Sorts four sets by color (Ex: blue, red, green, yellow blocks)									
Sorts two sets by shape (Ex: circles, squares)									
Sorts four sets by shape (Ex: circles, squares, ovals, stars)									
Sorts two sets by size (Ex: large combs, small combs)									
Sorts three sets by size (Ex: small, medium, large spoons)									

Comments: Items to be sorted should differ *only* in the characteristics selected.

Code: C = Correct, Independent
E = Emerging or Prompted
I = Incorrect or No Response

Staff Completing Assessment

____

Basic Skills Checklists © 2008 Marlene Breitenbach

Name: ______________________________ Grade: ____________________

Date(s) assessed: ____________________ School Year: ______________

Skill Area: SORTING (Two Variables) Targets:									
Sorts by color and shape (Ex: red and blue circles and stars; size does not differ)									
Sorts by color and size (Ex: large and small brown and blue combs; shape does not differ)									
Sorts by shape and size (Ex: large and small triangles and circles; color does not differ)									

Comments: Items to be sorted should differ *only* in the characteristics selected.

Code: C = Correct, Independent
E = Emerging or Prompted
I = Incorrect or No Response

Staff Completing Assessment

____

Basic Skills Checklists © 2008 Marlene Breitenbach

Basic Skills Checklist I

Name: ______________________________ **Grade:** ____________________

Date(s) assessed: ____________________ **School Year:** _______________

Skill Area: **COLORS** **Targets:**	**Match**	**Receptive ID**	**Expressive ID**	**Match word**	**Read word**	**Spell word**
red						
blue						
yellow						
green						
orange						
purple						
brown						
black						
white						
grey						
pink						

Comments:

Code: C = Correct, Independent
E = Emerging or Prompted
I = Incorrect or No Response

Staff Completing Assessment

____

Basic Skills Checklists © 2008 Marlene Breitenbach

Name: ______________________ Grade: ______________

Date(s) assessed: ______________ School Year: ____________

Skill Area: SHAPES Targets:	Match	Receptive ID	Expressive ID	Match word	Read word	Spell word
circle						
square						
triangle						
rectangle						
oval						
star						
diamond						
heart						
hexagon						

Comments:

Code: C = Correct, Independent
E = Emerging or Prompted
I = Incorrect or No Response

Staff Completing Assessment

____

Basic Skills Checklists © 2008 Marlene Breitenbach

Name: ______________________ Grade: ______________

Date(s) assessed: ______________ School Year: ______________

Skill Area: BODY PARTS I Targets:	Receptive	Expressive		Receptive	Expressive		Receptive	Expressive	
mouth									
eyes									
nose									
ears									
hair									
teeth									
chin									
tongue									
head									
foot									

Comments:

Code: C = Correct, Independent
E = Emerging or Prompted
I = Incorrect or No Response

Staff Completing Assessment

____

Basic Skills Checklists © 2008 Marlene Breitenbach

Name: ______________________ Grade: ______________________

Date(s) assessed: ______________________ School Year: ______________________

Skill Area: BODY PARTS Targets:	Receptive	Expressive		Receptive	Expressive		Receptive	Expressive	
hand									
legs									
arms									
fingers									
toes									
neck									
stomach									
back									
knee									
chest									

Comments:

Code: C = Correct, Independent
E = Emerging or Prompted
I = Incorrect or No Response

Staff Completing Assessment

____

Basic Skills Checklists © 2008 Marlene Breitenbach

Basic Skills Checklist I

Name: ______________________ Grade: ______________

Date(s) assessed: ______________ School Year: ______________

Skill Area: CATEGORIES Targets:	Foods	Animals	Toys	Vehicles	Clothing	People	Furniture	Tools	Numbers
Matches objects by category									
Sorts objects by category									
Matches pictures by category									
Sorts ten pictures by category									
Receptively identifies category: Ex: "Show me a [food]"									
Expressively identifies category: Ex: "What is a [cow]?"									
Names five items in a category: Ex: "Tell me some [foods]"									

Comments:

Code: C = Correct, Independent
E = Emerging or Prompted
I = Incorrect or No Response

Staff Completing Assessment

____

Basic Skills Checklists © 2008 Marlene Breitenbach

Basic Skills Checklist I/G

Name: ______________________________ Grade: ____________________

Date(s) assessed: ____________________ School Year: ______________

Skill Area: SEQUENCING Targets:									
Sequencing ("Put in order")									
Three-scene sequence									
Four-scene sequence									
Five-scene sequence									
Sequences five numbers									
Sequences five letters									
Identifies missing item in sequence									
Identify first - last									
Receptive ("Put x first")									
Receptive ("Put x last")									
Expressive ("Where is x?" - first)									
Expressive ("Where is x?" - last)									

Comments:

Code: C = Correct, Independent
E = Emerging or Prompted
I = Incorrect or No Response

Staff Completing Assessment

____

Basic Skills Checklists © 2008 Marlene Breitenbach

Name: ____________________ Grade: ____________________

Date(s) assessed: ____________________ School Year: ____________________

Skill Area: OPPOSITES Targets:	Receptive (objects)	Expressive (objects)	Receptive (pictures)	Expressive (pictures)
Opposites				
wet - dry				
hard - soft				
big - little				
thick - thin				
rough - smooth				
tall - short				
fat - thin				
long - short				
top - bottom				
front - back				
same - different				

Comments:
Receptive SD "Give me or point to [same/different]."
Expressive SD "Are these the [same/different]?"

Code: C = Correct, Independent
E = Emerging or Prompted
I = Incorrect or No Response

Staff Completing Assessment

____

Basic Skills Checklists © 2008 Marlene Breitenbach

Name: ____________________ Grade: ____________________

Date(s) assessed: ____________________ School Year: ____________________

Skill Area: PREPOSITIONS Targets:	Receptive (self)	Receptive (objects)	Receptive (pictures)	Expressive (self)	Expressive (objects)	Expressive (pictures)
Prepositions						
on						
under						
in						
behind						
in front						
next to						
inside						
between						
beside						
above						
over						

self = moves self to correct location or identifies where she/he is

object = moves object to or identifies correct location of object

picture = identifies correct location in pictures by pointing or describing location

Comments:

Code: C = Correct, Independent
E = Emerging or Prompted
I = Incorrect or No Response

Staff Completing Assessment

____

Basic Skills Checklists © 2008 Marlene Breitenbach

Basic Skills Checklist

I

Name: ______________________ Grade: ______________

Date(s) assessed: ______________ School Year: ______________

Skill Area: ALPHABET SKILLS Targets:	Recite alphabet to:	Sequence letters to:	Uppercase Receptive ID	Uppercase Expressive ID	Lowercase Receptive ID	Lowercase Expressive ID	Match Upper-Lowercase
A							
B							
C							
D							
E							
F							
G							
H							
I							
J							
K							
L							
M							
N							
O							

Comments:

Code: C = Correct, Independent
E = Emerging or Prompted
I = Incorrect or No Response

Staff Completing Assessment

____

Basic Skills Checklists © 2008 Marlene Breitenbach

Basic Skills Checklist

Name: ______________________________ Grade: ____________________

Date(s) assessed: ____________________ School Year: ______________

Skill Area: ALPHABET SKILLS II Targets:	Recite alphabet to:	Sequence letters to:	Uppercase Receptive ID	Uppercase Expressive ID	Lowercase Receptive ID	Lowercase Expressive ID	Match Upper-Lowercase
P							
Q							
R							
S							
T							
U							
V							
W							
X							
Y							
Z							

Comments:

Code: C = Correct, Independent
E = Emerging or Prompted
I = Incorrect or No Response

Staff Completing Assessment

____

Basic Skills Checklist

I

Name: ______________________ Grade: ______________________

Date(s) assessed: ______________________ School Year: ______________________

Skill Area: COMMUNITY SIGNS Targets:	Receptive ID	Expressive ID	Match word to sign	Give meaning
GO				
STOP				
IN				
OUT				
MEN'S				
WOMEN'S				
WASHROOMS				
RESTROOMS				
TOILETS				
ENTER				
EXIT				
LADIES				
GENTLEMEN				
POISON				
WALK				
CAUTION				
DANGER				

Comments:

Code: C = Correct, Independent
E = Emerging or Prompted
I = Incorrect or No Response

Staff Completing Assessment

____

Basic Skills Checklists © 2008 Marlene Breitenbach

Name: ____________________ Grade: ____________

Date(s) assessed: ____________________ School Year: ____________

Skill Area: DICTIONARY AND BOOK SKILLS Targets:									
Places letters in alphabetical order									
Places words in order by first letter									
Places words in order by second letter									
Places words in order by third letter									
Locates guide words in dictionary									
Uses guide words to find correct page									
Locates target word									
Selects correct definition									
Locates table of contents									
Locates title page									
Identifies title and author									
Locates index									

Comments:

Code: C = Correct, Independent
E = Emerging or Prompted
I = Incorrect or No Response

Staff Completing Assessment

____

Basic Skills Checklists © 2008 Marlene Breitenbach

Name: ______________________ Grade: ______________

Date(s) assessed: ______________ School Year: ____________

Skill Area: CAPITALIZATION & PUNCTUATION Targets:									
Capitalize:									
Beginning of sentence									
People's names									
Days of the week									
Months									
Holidays									
Cities									
Countries									
Titles of books									
Punctuation:									
Places period at the end of sentence									
Places comma between date/year									
Places comma between city/state									
Uses exclamation point appropriately									
Uses question mark appropriately									
Uses apostrophe appropriately									

Comments:

Skills may be assessed using a writing sample, dated and saved in student portfolio.

Code: C = Correct, Independent
E = Emerging or Prompted
I = Incorrect or No Response

Staff Completing Assessment

____

Basic Skills Checklists © 2008 Marlene Breitenbach

Name: ______________________ Grade: ______________

Date(s) assessed: ______________ School Year: ______________

MATH - NUMBER CONCEPTS Targets:	Rote counts to:	Receptive ID	Expressive ID	Sequences Numbers to:	Counts Objects to:	Matches Number to Quantity:	Adds 1 - 5 to:	Adds 6 - 9 to:
1								
2								
3								
4								
5								
6								
7								
8								
9								
10								
11								
12								
13								
14								
15								
16								
17								
18								
19								
20								

Code: C = Correct, Independent
E = Emerging or Prompted
I = Incorrect or No Response

Staff Completing Assessment

____

Basic Skills Checklists © 2008 Marlene Breitenbach

Name: ____________________ Grade: ____________

Date(s) assessed: ____________ School Year: ____________

Skill Area: **ADDITION** Targets:							
Single digit numbers 1-9							
Three single digit numbers 1-9							
Single digit number to double digit number							
Double digit numbers (no regrouping)							
Double digit numbers (one regrouping)							
Three digit numbers (no regrouping)							
Three digit numbers (one regrouping)							
Three digit numbers (two regroupings)							

Comments: Save dated independent work sample of each skill.

Code: C = Correct, Independent
E = Emerging or Prompted
I = Incorrect or No Response

Staff Completing Assessment

____

Basic Skills Checklists © 2008 Marlene Breitenbach

Name: ______________________ Grade: ______________

Date(s) assessed: ______________ School Year: ____________

Skill Area: SUBTRACTION Targets:							
Single digit numbers 1-9							
Double-digit numbers (no renaming)							
Double-digit numbers (one renaming)							
Three-digit numbers (no renaming)							
Three-digit numbers (one renaming)							
Three-digit numbers (two renamings)							

Comments: Save dated independent work sample of each skill.

Code: C = Correct, Independent
E = Emerging or Prompted
I = Incorrect or No Response

Staff Completing Assessment

____

Basic Skills Checklists © 2008 Marlene Breitenbach

Name: ____________________ **Grade:** ____________________

Date(s) assessed: ____________________ **School Year:** ____________________

Skill Area: CALENDAR SKILLS Targets:									
Recites days of the week									
Recites months of the year									
Recites the seasons									
Reads days of the week									
Reads months of the year									
Reads the seasons									
Sequences days of the week									
Sequences months of the year									
Sequences the seasons									
Locates days on a calendar									
Locates months on a calendar									
Locates birthday on a calendar									
Locates holidays on a calendar									

Comments:

Code: C = Correct, Independent
E = Emerging or Prompted
I = Incorrect or No Response

Staff Completing Assessment

____

Basic Skills Checklists © 2008 Marlene Breitenbach

Name: ____________________ Grade: ____________________

Date(s) assessed: ____________________ School Year: ____________________

Skill Area: TIME SKILLS Targets:									
identifies minute hand									
identifies hour hand									
reads time to the hour									
reads time to the half hour									
reads time to the quarter hour									
reads time in five minute intervals									
reads time in one minute intervals									
understands concept of today									
understands concept of yesterday									
understands concept of tomorrow									
knows number of days in a week									
knows number of days in a year									
knows number of weeks in a year									
knows number of months in a year									

Comments:

Code: C = Correct, Independent
E = Emerging or Prompted
I = Incorrect or No Response

Staff Completing Assessment

____

Basic Skills Checklists © 2008 Marlene Breitenbach

Name: ______________________ Grade: ______________________

Date(s) assessed: ______________________ School Year: ______________________

Skill Area: MONEY SKILLS Targets:	Receptive	Expressive		Receptive	Expressive		Receptive	Expressive	
identifies:									
penny									
nickel									
dime									
quarter									
loonie (Canada)									
toonie (Canada)									
half dollar									
dollar									
identifies value of:									
penny									
nickel									
dime									
quarter									
loonie (Canada)									
toonie (Canada)									
half dollar									
dollar									

Comments:

Code: C = Correct, Independent
E = Emerging or Prompted
I = Incorrect or No Response

Staff Completing Assessment

____

Basic Skills Checklists © 2008 Marlene Breitenbach

Name: ______________________ Grade: ______________

Date(s) assessed: ______________ School Year: ____________

Skill Area: MEASUREMENT SKILLS Targets:									
measure (linear)									
1 inch									
5 inches									
½ inch									
¼ inch									
1 foot									
1 yard									
1 centimeter									
1 meter									
10 centimeters									
measure (liquid)									
1 cup									
½ cup									
¼ cup									
2 ounces									
4 ounces									

Comments:

Code: C = Correct, Independent
E = Emerging or Prompted
I = Incorrect or No Response

Staff Completing Assessment

____

Basic Skills Checklists © 2008 Marlene Breitenbach

Basic Skills Checklist I/G

Name: ______________________________ Grade: ____________________

Date(s) assessed: ____________________ School Year: ________________

Skill Area: FUNCTIONAL HAND SKILLS Targets:									
Opens thermos									
Closes thermos									
Opens milk / juice container									
Closes milk / juice container									
Opens plastic ware									
Closes plastic ware									
Opens jar									
Closes jar									
Turns doorknob to open									
Uses paper towel dispenser									
Unwraps food (foil, baggie)									
Opens wrapper (straw, candy)									
Opens lunch box									
Closes lunch box									
Opens kitbag or knapsack									
Closes kitbag or knapsack									

Comments:

Code: C = Correct, Independent
E = Emerging or Prompted
I = Incorrect or No Response

Staff Completing Assessment

____

Basic Skills Checklists © 2008 Marlene Breitenbach

Basic Skills Checklist I/G

Name: ______________________ Grade: ______________

Date(s) assessed: ______________ School Year: ______________

Skill Area: MANIPULATIVE PLAY Targets:									
Turns knobs on toys									
Winds up toys									
Activates push-button toys									
Builds block tower (# of pieces)									
Imitates block structure									
Completes * inset puzzle (# of pieces)									
Completes ** non-inset puzzle (# of pieces)									
Pulls apart construction toys									
Completes lacing sequence (5 holes)									
Strings 5 items									
Fills pegboard									
Pounds/squeezes playdoh									

Comments: Insert response code and # of pieces (e.g., C/10).
*inset puzzle = frame around single or all pieces
**non-inset puzzle = no frame around single or all pieces

Code: C = Correct, Independent
E = Emerging or Prompted
I = Incorrect or No Response

Staff Completing Assessment

____

Name: ______________________________ Grade: ____________________

Date(s) assessed: ____________________ School Year: ________________

Skill Area: CLOTHING MANAGEMENT I Targets:									
Buttons large buttons 2"									
Unbuttons large buttons 2"									
Buttons small buttons 1/2"									
Unbuttons small buttons 1/2"									
Unsnaps									
Snaps									
Snaps pants									
Unzips zipper									
Zips up zipper									
Attaches zipper at bottom									
Zips pants									
Buckles belt									
Unties shoes									
Ties shoes									
Laces shoes									

Comments:

Code: C = Correct, Independent
E = Emerging or Prompted
I = Incorrect or No Response

Staff Completing Assessment

____

Basic Skills Checklists © 2008 Marlene Breitenbach

Name: ______________________ Grade: ______________

Date(s) assessed: ______________________ School Year: ______________

Skill Area: CLOTHING MANAGEMENT II Targets:									
Hangs shirt on hanger									
Hangs jacket on clothes hook									
Hangs item with clothes pins									
Folds washcloth									
Folds hand towel									
Folds bath towel									
Folds pants									
Folds shirts									
Matches socks									
Identifies front and back of clothing									
Turns clothes right-side-out									

Comments:

Code: C = Correct, Independent
E = Emerging or Prompted
I = Incorrect or No Response

Staff Completing Assessment

____

Basic Skills Checklists © 2008 Marlene Breitenbach

Basic Skills Checklist I/G

Name: ______________________ Grade: ______________________

Date(s) assessed: ______________________ School Year: ______________________

Skill Area: ART SKILLS I Targets:									
Picks up / holds scissors correctly									
Snips with child's scissors									
Cuts across 1" paper strip									
Cuts on 4" straight line									
Cuts out simple shapes (circle, square, triangle)									
Cuts out complex shapes (star, tree, flower)									
Glues paper to paper									
Glues shape to outline									
Folds paper in half									
Manipulates Play-Doh									

Comments: Note if adaptive or loop scissors are needed.

Code: C = Correct, Independent
E = Emerging or Prompted
I = Incorrect or No Response

Staff Completing Assessment

____

Basic Skills Checklist **I/G**

Name: ______________________ **Grade:** ______________

Date(s) assessed: ______________ **School Year:** ____________

Skill Area: ART SKILLS II Targets:									
Paints at easel									
Paints on paper									
Paints recognizable item									
Scribbles with crayons									
Colors within lines (simple shapes)									
Colors within lines (complex shapes)									
Draws familiar objects/people									
Uses a ruler									
Follows picture directions or copies sample (art project or worksheet)									
Follows written directions (art project or worksheet)									
Follows verbal directions (art project or worksheet)									

Comments:

Code: C = Correct, Independent
E = Emerging or Prompted
I = Incorrect or No Response

Staff Completing Assessment

____

Basic Skills Checklists © 2008 Marlene Breitenbach

Name: ______________________ Grade: ______________

Date(s) assessed: ______________ School Year: ______________

Skill Area: PRE-WRITING Targets:									
Uses fisted grasp									
Uses pincer grasp									
Uses tripod grasp									
Fills in simple shape stencil									
Fills in complex shape stencil									
Connects dots									
Traces lines									
Traces curves									
Traces shapes									
Traces letters									

Comments: Note if pencil adapter is used.

Code: C = Correct, Independent
E = Emerging or Prompted
I = Incorrect or No Response

Staff Completing Assessment

____

Basic Skills Checklists © 2008 Marlene Breitenbach

Basic Skills Checklist

I/G

Name: ______________________ Grade: ______________________

Date(s) assessed: ______________________ School Year: ______________________

Skill Area: WRITING Targets:									
Imitates* lines (I , — , T)									
Imitates lines (/ , \ , X)									
Imitates curves (C, U, O)									
Imitates letters									
Copies ** lines (I , — , T, / , \ , X)									
Copies straight line letters									
Copies curved line letters									
Copies numbers									
Writes letters from dictation									
Writes numbers from dictation									
Copies name									
Writes name									

Comments:
* imitate = student watches you write, then writes the same
** copy = student is given a written sample and writes the same

Code: C = Correct, Independent
E = Emerging or Prompted
I = Incorrect or No Response

Staff Completing Assessment

____

Basic Skills Checklists © 2008 Marlene Breitenbach

Name: ______________________ Grade: ______________

Date(s) assessed: ______________ School Year: ______________

Skill Area: CLERICAL I Targets:									
Stuffs envelopes									
Stamps envelope									
Attaches mailing labels									
Uses stapler									
Uses staple remover									
Uses single-hole punch									
Uses three-hole punch									
Uses pencil sharpener									
Attaches paper clip									
Collates three pieces									
Uses copy machine									
Wraps items with rubber band									

Comments:

Code: C = Correct, Independent
E = Emerging or Prompted
I = Incorrect or No Response

Staff Completing Assessment

____

Basic Skills Checklists © 2008 Marlene Breitenbach

Name: ____________________ Grade: ____________________

Date(s) assessed: ____________________ School Year: ____________________

Skill Area: CLERICAL II Targets:									
Files by color									
Files letters in order (A - Z)									
Files numbers in order (1-25)									
Files by ZIP or postal code									
Files words by first letter									
Files words by second letter									
Files by last name									

Comments:

Code: C = Correct, Independent
E = Emerging or Prompted
I = Incorrect or No Response

Staff Completing Assessment

____

Basic Skills Checklists © 2008 Marlene Breitenbach

Name: ______________________ Grade: ______________

Date(s) assessed: ______________ School Year: ______________

Skill Area: SCHOOL SKILLS I Targets:									
Exits bus									
Transitions to school entryway									
Opens door									
Transitions to classroom									
Removes and hangs up jacket									
Hangs up bag or backpack									
Changes shoes									
Locates own desk									
Waits in line with peers for 2 minutes									
Waits in line with peers for 4 minutes									
Walks with a peer during transitions									
Transitions to lunchroom									
Gets items needed for lunch									
Cleans up after lunch									
Throws away trash									

Comments:

Code: C = Correct, Independent
E = Emerging or Prompted
I = Incorrect or No Response

Staff Completing Assessment

____

Basic Skills Checklist

I/G

Name: ______________________ Grade: ______________________

Date(s) assessed: ______________________ School Year: ______________________

Skill Area: SCHOOL SKILLS II Targets:									
Transitions to playground for recess									
Plays outside with peers 3-5 minutes									
Plays outside with peers 5-10 minutes									
Responds to peer invitation to play									
Asks to join play with others									
Responds to greetings from peers									
Responds to greetings from adults									
Follows one-step group directions									
Follows two-step group directions									
Delivers paper message to other school location									
Delivers verbal message to other school location									
Completes one worksheet or assigned task									
Completes two assigned tasks									

Comments:

Code: C = Correct, Independent
E = Emerging or Prompted
I = Incorrect or No Response

Staff Completing Assessment

____

Name: ______________________ Grade: ______________

Date(s) assessed: ______________ School Year: ______________

Skill Area: SCHOOL SKILLS III Targets:									
Sits near peers appropriately									
Attends to story five minutes									
Attends to story ten minutes									
Attends to lecture five minutes									
Attends to lecture ten minutes									
Raises hand to request assistance									
Raises hand to request a turn									
Raises hand to answer questions									
Shares materials									
Works cooperatively in small groups									

Comments:

Code: C = Correct, Independent
E = Emerging or Prompted
I = Incorrect or No Response

Staff Completing Assessment

____

Basic Skills Checklist

Name: ______________________________ Grade: ____________________

School Year: ______________

Schedule Format:

☐ half day
☐ whole day
☐ single task
☐ multiple task
☐ other ________

☐ clipboard
☐ binder
☐ file folder
☐ checklist
☐ other ____________

Stimulus Used:

☐ object
☐ photo
☐ picture symbol
☐ text
number of visible schedule items _____

Date(s) assessed:

Skill Area: SCHEDULE USE Targets:				
DAILY SCHEDULE				
reacts to transition signal or direction				
looks at schedule to identify next activity				
moves to next activity or setting				
places schedule in correct storage location				
removes schedule card after finished				
ACTIVITY SCHEDULE				
points to schedule card or picture				
retrieves items need for task				
sets up and completes task				
returns items to shelf				

Comments:

Code: C = Correct, Independent
E = Emerging or Prompted
I = Incorrect or No Response

Staff Completing Assessment

____

Basic Skills Checklist I

Name: ______________________ Grade: ______________

Date(s) assessed: ______________ School Year: ______________

Sample Tasks:

Skill Area: WORK SKILLS Targets:	Assembly (2 pc)	Assembly (3 pc)	Assembly (4 pc)	Packaging (2 pc)	Packaging (3 pc)	Packaging (4 pc)	
Gets needed materials							
Sets up task in correct order							
Completes task							
Asks for help if needed							
Indicates when finished							
Puts away materials							
Assembly Task Examples:							
2 pc (pencil/eraser)							
3 pc (nut, bolt, washer)							
4 pc. (Lego car)							
Packaging Task Examples:							
2 pc (tops/bottoms-box/canister)							
3 pc (toothbrush holders/toothbrush)							
4 pc. (School supplies/pencil case)							

Comments:

Code: C = Correct, Independent
E = Emerging or Prompted
I = Incorrect or No Response

Staff Completing Assessment

____

Basic Skills Checklists © 2008 Marlene Breitenbach

Name: ______________________ Grade: ______________

Date(s) assessed: ______________ School Year: ______________

Skill Area: HOME / SCHOOL JOBS Targets:									
Sets table									
Clears table									
Wipes table									
Separates trash / non-trash									
Sorts recyclables									
Washes dishes									
Dries dishes									
Puts away tableware									
Sorts silverware									
Sweeps small area									
Waters plants									
Dusts surfaces									
Washes mirror									
Feeds pets									
Carries items on a tray									

Comments:

Code: C = Correct, Independent
E = Emerging or Prompted
I = Incorrect or No Response

Staff Completing Assessment

____

Basic Skills Checklists © 2008 Marlene Breitenbach

Basic Skills Parent Checklist

Name: ______________________________ **Date:** ____________________

Please check the column that indicates your child's current skill in each area.

Skill Area: EATING Targets:	Needs Help	Independent	No Opportunity
Holds glass			
Eats with fingers			
Uses spoon			
Uses fork			
Uses straw			
Uses knife to spread			
Uses knife to cut			
Uses knife to peel			
Prepares toast			
Prepares cereal			
Prepares sandwich			
Uses microwave			

Comments:

Caregiver Completing Assessment

____

Basic Skills Checklists © 2008 Marlene Breitenbach

Basic Skills Parent Checklist

Name: ______________________________ Date: ____________________

Please check the column that indicates your child's current skill in each area.

Skill Area: GROOMING Targets:	Needs Help	Independent	No Opportunity
Puts toothpaste on brush			
Brushes teeth			
Turns faucets on /off			
Washes face			
Dries face			
Washes hands			
Dries hands			
Bathes self			
Shampoos hair			
Combs/brushes hair			
Prepares cereal			
Wipes/blows nose			

Comments:

Caregiver Completing Assessment

____

Basic Skills Parent Checklist

Name: ______________________________ Date: ______________________

Please check the column that indicates your child's current skill in each area.

Skill Area: DRESSING I Targets:	Needs Help	Independent	No Opportunity
Undressing			
Removes socks			
Removes shoes			
Removes jacket			
Removes shirt			
Removes dress			
Removes "pullover" garments			
Dressing			
Puts on shoes			
Puts on socks			
Puts on shirt			
Puts on dress			
Puts on jacket			
Puts on shoes			

Comments:

Caregiver Completing Assessment

____

Basic Skills Parent Checklist

Name: ______________________________ Date: ____________________

Please check the column that indicates your child's current skill in each area.

Skill Area: DRESSING II Targets:	Needs Help	Independent	No Opportunity
Dressing			
Puts shoes on correct feet			
Puts on "pullover garments"			
Dresses self			
Knows back and front of clothes			
Recognizes if inside-out and turns			
Fasteners			
Closes snaps			
Opens snaps			
Unbuttons and buttons 1" buttons			
Unbuttons and buttons ½" buttons			
Starts zipper			
Zips and unzips			
Ties shoes			

Comments:

Caregiver Completing Assessment

____

Basic Skills Checklists © 2008 Marlene Breitenbach

Basic Skills Parent Checklist

Name: ______________________________ Date: ____________________

Please check the column that indicates your child's current skill in each area.

Skill Area: TOILETING Targets:	Sometimes	Always	Never
Indicates when wet or soiled			
Verbalizes toilet need			
Communicates toilet need nonverbally*			
Initiates without reminders			
Urinates in toilet			
Has bowel movement in toilet			
Manipulates clothing to use the toilet			
Wipes self			
Flushes			
Washes hands after toileting			
Has urination accidents (how often?)			
Has bowel accidents (how often?)			
Remains dry at night			

Comments:
*Please describe:

Caregiver Completing Assessment

____

Basic Skills Parent Checklist

Name: ________________________________ Date: ______________________

Please check the column that indicates your child's current skill in each area.

Skill Area: DOMESTIC I Targets:	Needs Help	Independent	No Opportunity
Wipes up spills			
Sets table			
Clears table			
Washes dishes			
Dries dishes			
Puts away dishes			
Puts away toys			
Makes bed			
Sweeps floor			
Folds clothes			
Puts away clothes			

Comments:

Caregiver Completing Assessment

____

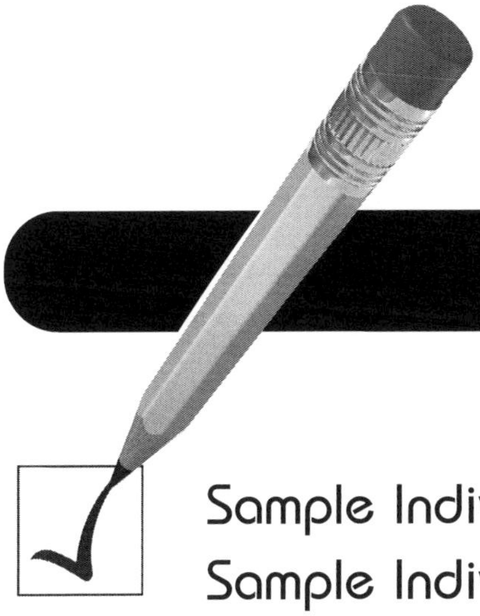

APPENDIX

SAMPLE INDIVIDUAL CHECKLIST

I

Name: ______________________ Grade: ______________________

Date(s) assessed: ______________________ School Year: ______________________

MATH - NUMBER CONCEPTS Targets:	Rote counts to:	Receptive ID	Expressive ID	Sequences Numbers to:	Count Objects to:	Matches Number to Quantity:	Adds 1 - 5 to:	Adds 6 - 9 to:
1	C	C	C	C	C	C		
2	C	C	C	C	C	C		
3	C	C	C	C	C	I		
4	C	C	C	I	C	I		
5	C	C	C	I	C	I		
6	C	C	C	I	I			
7	C	C	C	I	I			
8	C	C	I	I	I			
9	C	C	I	I	I			
10	C	C	C	I	I			
11	C	C	I	I				
12	C	C	I	I				
13	C	C	I	I				
14	C	C	I	I				
15	C	C	I	I				
16	C	C	I	I				
17	C	C	I	I				
18	C	C	I	I				
19	C	C	C	I				
20	C	C	C	I				

Code: C = Correct, Independent
E = Emerging or Prompted
I = Incorrect or No Response

Staff Completing Assessment

____

SAMPLE INDIVIDUAL CHECKLIST

I

Name: ______________________________ Grade: ____________________

Date(s) assessed: ____________________ School Year: ________________

Skill Area: ALPHABET SKILLS Targets:	Recites alphabet to:	Sequences letters to:	Uppercase Receptive ID	Uppercase Expressive ID	Lowercase Receptive ID	Lowercase Expressive ID	Match Upper-Lowercase
A	C	C	C	C	I		
B	C	C	C	I	I		
C	C	C	C	C	C		
D	C	C	C	C	I		
E	C	C	C	C	I		
F	C	C	C	I	I		
G	C	C	C	I	I		
H	C	C	C	I	I		
I	C	C	C	I	I		
J	C	C	C	C	C		
K	C	C	C	C	C		
L	C	C	C	C	C		
M	C	C	C	I	I		
N	C	C	C	I	I		
O	C	C	C	C	C		

Comments:

Code: C = Correct, Independent
E = Emerging or Prompted
I = Incorrect or No Response

Staff Completing Assessment

____

SAMPLE GROUP ADMINISTRATION CHECKLIST **I/G**

Name: ______________________________ Grade: ____________________

Date(s) assessed: ____________________ School Year: ________________

Skill Area: ART SKILLS I Targets:	John	Brad	Katie	Matthew	Darcy	Louise			
Picks up / holds scissors correctly	C	I	C	C	C	E			
Snips with child's scissors	C	I	C	C	C	I			
Cuts across 1" paper strip	C	I	C	E	E	I			
Cuts on 4" straight line	E	I	C	I	I	I			
Cuts out simple shapes (circle, square, triangle)	I	I	E	I	I	I			
Cuts out complex shapes (star, tree, flower)	I	I	I	I	I	I			
Glues paper to paper	E	E	C	C	C	E			
Glues shape to outline	I	I	C	C	C	E			
Folds paper in half	I	I	C	I	I	I			
Manipulates Play-Doh	C	C	C	C	I	C			

Comments: Note if adaptive or loop scissors are needed.

Code: C = Correct, Independent
E = Emerging or Prompted
I = Incorrect or No Response

Staff Completing Assessment

____

Basic Skills Checklists © 2008 Marlene Breitenbach

Basic Skills Checklist

I

Name: ______________________

Grade: ______________

School Year: ______________

Schedule Format:

- ☐ half day
- ■ whole day
- ☐ single task
- ■ multiple task
- ☐ other ________
- ■ clipboard
- ☐ binder
- ☐ file folder
- ☐ checklist
- ☐ other ____________

Stimulus Used:

- ☐ object
- ☐ photo
- ■ picture symbol
- ☐ text

number of visible schedule items 8

Skill Area: SCHEDULE USE Targets:	9/20/06	11/22/06	2/15/07	5/25/07
DAILY SCHEDULE				
reacts to transition signal or direction	E	C	C	C
looks at schedule to identify next activity	I	C	C	C
moves to next activity or setting	E	C	C	C
places schedule in correct storage location	I	E	C	C
removes schedule card after finished	I	E	E	C
ACTIVITY SCHEDULE				
points to schedule card or picture	I	I	E	C
retrieves items need for task	E	C	C	C
sets up and completes task	E	E	C	C
returns items to shelf	E	C	C	C

Comments:

Code: C = Correct, Independent
E = Emerging or Prompted
I = Incorrect or No Response

Staff Completing Assessment

____

Basic Skills Checklists © 2008 Marlene Breitenbach

Basic Skills Checklist

I

Name: ______________________________ Grade: ____________________

Date(s) assessed: ____________________ School Year: ________________

Skill Area: Targets:							

Comments:

Code: C = Correct, Independent
E = Emerging or Prompted
I = Incorrect or No Response

Staff Completing Assessment

____

Basic Skills Checklists © 2008 Marlene Breitenbach

Basic Skills Parent Checklist

Name: ______________________________ **Date:** ____________________

Please check the column that indicates your child's current skill in each area.

Skill Area: **Targets:**	**Needs Help**	**Independent**	**No Opportunity**

Comments:

Caregiver Completing Assessment

____

Basic Skills Checklists © 2008 Marlene Breitenbach